The STAR Method Explained

PROVEN TECHNIQUE
TO SUCCEED AT INTERVIEW

Martha Gage

© Copyright 2019 by Martha Gage

All rights reserved.

The content contained within this book may not be reproduced, duplicated or transmitted without direct written permission from the author or the publisher.

Under no circumstances will any blame or legal responsibility be held against the publisher, or author, for any damages, reparation, or monetary loss due to the information contained within this book. Either directly or indirectly.

Legal Notice:

This book is copyright protected. This book is only for personal use. You cannot amend, distribute, sell, use, quote or paraphrase any part, or the content within this book, without the consent of the author or publisher.

Disclaimer Notice:

Please note the information contained within this document is for educational and entertainment purposes only. All effort has been executed to present accurate, up to date, and reliable, complete information. No warranties of any kind are declared or implied. Readers acknowledge that the author is not engaging in the rendering of legal, financial, medical or professional advice. The content within this book has been derived from various sources. Please consult a licensed professional before attempting any techniques outlined in this book.

By reading this document, the reader agrees that under no circumstances is the author responsible for any losses, direct or indirect, which are incurred as a result of the use of information contained within this document, including, but not limited to, — errors, omissions, or inaccuracies.

ISBN: 9781097832057

TABLE OF CONTENTS

Introduction..4

CHAPTER 1: Employer Priorities...6

CHAPTER 2: Creating a Measurable Difference........................11

CHAPTER 3: Communicating a Measurable Difference..........18

CHAPTER 4: STAR Framework...24

CHAPTER 5: Action Verbs Tell a Story..29

CHAPTER 6: Interview Questions and Answers.......................36

CHAPTER 7: Creating Your STAR Resume.................................57

CHAPTER 8: STAR Cover Letters...64

Conclusion..71

INTRODUCTION

Welcome and thank you for your purchase of "The Star Method Explained." In this book you will learn about STAR framework and how it can assist you in behavioral questions in interviews and more! The topics covered will be:

- **Employer Priorities:** Getting you in the proper mindset for learning the process by assuming the role of Interviewer. What sort of answers would you want to hear if you were asking the same questions day after day?
- **Creating a Measurable Difference:** In this chapter, we go further into a winning interview mindset by taking the time to chronicle and sort your skills and work experiences in preparation for STAR!
- **Communicating a Measurable Difference:** Here you will learn how to take experiences and select key stories for use in interviews.
- **STAR Framework:** Now that we've assessed ourselves, we are ready to learn the STAR system. No more nervous interviews!
- **Action Verbs Tell a Story:** Enhance your stories with action verbs to give them that extra zing.

- **Interview Questions and Answers:** We have compiled a list of some of the most popular of those tricky questions you might get during interviews. This will give you a chance to see what your STAR lessons lead to as you respond.
- **Creating Your STAR Resume:** How to bring that STAR power to your resume.
- **STAR Cover Letters:** How to write cover letters that will MAKE them want to read your resume!

We will provide examples along the way to start building a strong foundation. If it seems complicated at first, don't worry, because we have you covered. Stick with us and follow our tips and examples and you will be using the STAR system to your benefit in no time.

Take notes as you go along and you will have the basics of this system down. After that, start targeting the job that you have been dreaming of and don't be nervous about the interview.

Why worry about interviews, anyways? You've got a shining STAR!

CHAPTER 1: EMPLOYER PRIORITIES

You have been interviewed before, of course. You know the range of questions can be both alarming and disarming, but have you considered things from the side of the Interviewers?

For them, interviewing can be a somewhat tedious process. Asking some of the same questions over and over, noting the responses that stick out… and that is what we want to focus on in this chapter. Putting yourself in the interviewer's shoes. This way you can get a chance to modify your perspective a little and to try to ask yourself, "What would I be looking for? What information is interesting, relevant, and valuable?" It is a valuable little exercise.

We are going to start with things you should avoid saying during interviews and then move on to answers that interviewers enjoy hearing, so we can give you some contrast and a better understanding of what your words are really saying about you!

Do's and Don'ts in an interview

Let's see what you, as an interviewer, would prefer to hear. We have compiled some common questions that you have probably heard in many interviews. Assuming you are a

Team Leader or Manager tasked with interviewing, which answers might cause alarm bells to go off in your head?

1. **Question:** "What is your biggest weakness?"

Response 1: "I think that my biggest weakness is that I work too hard."

Response 2: "I haven't had any formal training in leadership, so sometimes I feel nervous when I've been given authority."

As an Interviewer, you might smile when you hear the first response but you'll probably be more likely to hire the second responder. The goal of this question is to determine if you have an accurate and realistic understanding of your strengths and weaknesses. Everyone has a weakness. Be honest about skills you would like to develop and be sure to have an answer or two ready for this question.

2. **Question:** "What did you like least about your last job?"

Response 1: "They were a bad company. I never got time off and the managers there don't know what they are doing."

Response 2: "My commute to work took a very long time."

This is a question that you have to answer carefully. As an Interviewer, if you heard someone badmouthing their previous company, what would you feel the chances of them doing the same to your own should they interview somewhere else? As an Interviewer something innocuous like Response 2 is certainly preferable, no?

3. **Question:** "Why should we hire you?"

Response 1: "I don't know. I think that I could do a good job and I work hard."

Response 2: "I like working with people and so I think that I'd be a great fit for customer service."

As an Interviewer you might ask this question 20 times in one day. Wouldn't you rather hear from an applicant that have considered the position they are trying for and determined why they want it?

4. **Question:** "Can you tell me a little about yourself?"

Response 1: "Well, I like video games and travelling. I read a lot and my favorite food is pizza."

Response 2: "I've worked as a customer service representative for the last 5 years and one of my specialties is dealing with difficult customers."

As an Interviewer, Response 2 is going to be a lot more relevant for what you are hoping to accomplish. While you probably wouldn't mind a little personal information, if it is combined with work experience, you probably don't want to hear the applicants life story.

5. **Question:** "Do you work well with others?"

Response 1: "I think that I am. My last team didn't like me but I think they were just intimidated by my work style. I'm sure that I'll fit right in here."

Response 2: "I feel that I do. I try to make an effort to learn and use everyone's name quickly to establish rapport. I'm also a good listener and my priority is getting the job done, not getting the credit."

Response 1 would likely not be hearing back from you. After all, wouldn't you wonder how one person alienated a whole team? Response 2, however, has their priorities straight. Wouldn't you agree?

6. **Question:** "Do you have any questions that you would like to ask me?"

Response 1: "Will I have to work overtime a lot? Also, do we get any sort of employee discount?"

Response 2: "Do you have internal training available, in case I would like to expand my role in the company at some time in the future?"

This is a question you have heard before in an interview. As many times as people have heard it, it seems that no one has taken the time to prepare good answers. It is likely that you found Response number 2 a lot more refreshing.

Now that we have given you a little perspective as to what things are like on the side of the Interviewer, we are going to expand on this and tell you how you can prepare for questions like this and more. This will help you to make a measurable difference in the kind of first impressions you want to deliver.

After all, now that you've adopted the mindset and frustrations of an Interviewer, what better next step could there be than analyzing your own career history and experiences so you can ensure all your interview experiences are stellar?

Let's get ready to craft our own personal stories and then we'll introduce you to STAR. Are you ready? Let's proceed!

CHAPTER 2: CREATING A MEASURABLE DIFFERENCE

Our next step in putting yourself in the right mindset is going to be creating a breakdown of your current resume so we can extract individual skills. For example, many customer service resume entries are similar to these:

Supreme Project Planning — Budget analyst and Technical advisor — Apr. 2018-Current

Duties consisted of allocating resources for the implementation of projects. Retrofit data was analyzed in order to gain approval for upgrades.

Gravitas ISP — Customer Service Representative — Apr. 2017-Apr. 2018

Duties consisted of providing customer service and basic troubleshooting in a busy call center environment for customers using our internet service provider.

Looks pretty straightforward, no? Think about it a little harder, though. Are we encompassing all of the skills that this job takes? Not by a long shot. Let's make a list of some associated skills as an exercise. You may only use a fraction of them when we get to the portion of crafting a STAR resume but having a list can be the difference between night and day when you want to know exactly the right words to say.

Customer Service Skills terms

1. **Empathy** — Communicating effectively requires being able to put yourself in the customer's shoes. Whether it comes natural to you or not, this is a definite skill that you want mentioned for prospective employers.

2. **Leading a call** — Being able to lead the conversation helps to ensure that time is not being wasted and that clients may be pushed toward solutions for their issues more quickly. This is a very valuable skill.

3. **Time management** — Keeping productive in the face of a busy schedule is impossible without good time management skills. Be sure to list this as it is very important.

4. **Diplomacy** — A must in customer service. Not every customer is going to be easygoing and agreeable, having diplomacy skills means these customers are not an issue.

5. **Problem solving** — Solving problems is another major part of customer service. It could be assisting with company hardware or software or even the taming of difficult clients. If more on the technical side,

'troubleshooting' is a good word to use to communicate this skill.

6. **Product knowledge** — Be sure to list specialized skills that are particular to jobs you have worked. Particular call center software, for instance. Any software or hardware in which you have specialized training should always be mentioned.

7. **Speaking Professionally** — Keeping all conversations with clients and co-workers strictly professional is a useful skill that bears mention. You'd be surprised at how many people never quite pick it up!

8. **'Putting a smile in your voice'** — Another customer service gem. Smiling when you are speaking is a psychological trick that works. People can genuinely hear the smile in your words.

9. **Setting expectations** — A large percentages of cases where customers were dissatisfied with service has involved failing to set their expectations. If this is one of your skills, be sure to mention it.

10. **Closing calls** — Properly closing out calls after ensuring the needs of the customer have been met is a bit of an art form. If you are good at this, be sure to mention it!

Technical support skill terms

1. **Troubleshooting** — Problem solving on the tech side, this is one of the more common action verbs you can find on a resume.

2. **Engineered** — Engineering solutions is a common skill for a technician, don't forget to list it!.

3. **Programmed** — If you are a coder, this should be on your resume!

4. **Developed** — Used sometimes in lieu of engineering; solutions you've helped to develop or developed on your own should be listed as part of your skills set.

5. **Retrofit** — Upgrading existing technology to meet with today's standards; retrofit sounds nice and sharp on a resume so consider adding this one.

6. **Maintained** — Supporting a local technology infrastructure is considered 'maintaining' it. Use this one in a flash; the person who keeps everything running for the others should get credit for it.

7. **Generated** — This can be used in a number of ways. You generated interest in sales. You've generated a solution. Give it a try and see.

8. **Administered** — Were you managing systems on a network? Congratulations, you've administered systems! This is a much sought-after skill so don't do yourself the disservice of leaving it out.

9. **Standardized** — Often technology in a business environment needs to be upgraded to meet certain industry standards. This is what it means if you standardized an infrastructure.

10. **Researched** — Sometimes you need to compare software types or solutions the company is considering, why not list this among your skills?

Financial skills terms

1. **Budgeted** — If you have budgeted projects for your company, be sure to use this as a similar action verb (and we will delve into action verbs a bit more in Chapter 5).

2. **Allocated** — When determining which assets need to go where, you find yourself allocating resources. Say exactly that with this action verb.

3. **Analyzed** — If you have compared costs and what cuts need to be made, you've analyzed resources.

4. **Audited** — Before changes may be implemented an 'audit phase' is a common part of any plan. Don't forget to list it.

5. **Estimated** — Cost projection involves a lot of estimations so you will be using this word. Find a way to fit it in if you feel it applies in your skill collection.

6. **Reconciled** — Finding a hole in a budget is on par with anything a troubleshooter does in tech. Wading into the numbers and finding out the cause of discrepancies, well, that's one of the many reasons why you are an expert. Put it on that resume!

7. **Accounted** — Accounting for initial costs, accounting for pitfalls, accounting for contingencies. People fail to appreciate the planning, sometimes, but not in your line of work. There is nothing wrong with showing you are thorough in your resume and you kept things accounted for.

8. **Projected** — Future costs must be anticipated for any chance of a project to run properly. This is not a skill to neglect to mention.

9. **Inventoried** — You have to know what you have before you know what you need. Don't neglect to pay respect to your inventory skills.

10. **Identified** — Identifying solutions or potential pitfalls is a big part of handling the all-important budget. Don't forget to show off your foresight.

Use these and similar words. Make a list of skills you might be neglecting in your resume. The end-product is still intended to be short and sweet but getting into this practice can help ensure you don't leave anything important out during the process!

CHAPTER 3: COMMUNICATING A MEASURABLE DIFFERENCE

At its core, the STAR method is about telling a story. It's your story, actually. This means our next step is going to be the beginning of your story collection. After all, quantifying your skills is not enough. We need to make a list of stories so if you are asked the same question by other interviewers, you will have a different one for each. This will help interviewers to remember you as they compare notes and discuss your answers.

So, let's get started! We're going to take our 2 faux resume entries from the previous chapter and deduce some stories we might use from our skill sets.

We'll start with this one:

Gravitas ISP — Customer Service Representative — Apr. 2017–Apr. 2018

Duties consisted of providing customer service and basic troubleshooting in a busy call center environment for customers using our internet service provider.

We'll use this as your previous job. The new job that you are applying for has much the same type of employment, with a heavier technical background. Thus, it would be a good move up for you. Now that you have collected your skills, you are going to want to be able to apply them to personal stories. Let's take 3 common interview questions and a few selections from our previous skills listed and see what sort of answers this forethought tends to produce.

Highlighted skills

- A 'smile in your voice.'
- Troubleshooting.
- Diplomacy.
- Engineering solutions.
- Professional speaking.

1. **"What are you looking for in a new position?"**

"I'm looking for an environment where I can grow my technical skills while still getting to work with people. I started off in customer service and didn't know before that how much I would like working with people. Once I learned to put a smile in my voice and how to apply my technical training to troubleshooting I decided that this is the type of job for me."

2. **"How do you deal with stressful situations?"**

"Customer service taught me the value of diplomacy and keeping things on a professional level. As long as I keep my speaking professional I find that stress is not a personal thing. It keeps me focused on the job.'

3. **'Tell me about a challenge that you've faced at work and how you dealt with it.**"

"We had a customer who was frustrated with his web-authoring software, which is provided by our company. With patience, I got him to calm down a little and to tell me about the specific functionality he was wanting. We were able to engineer a solution at this point, as it turned out the feature which he wanted was available in an add-on to our software. I got him to try our demo version of the product so he could continue his work and he ended up buying the add-on!"

As you can see, by breaking down your skills into stories you have pre-rehearsed, interviews can become much easier. The stories don't have to be complicated, they just need to demonstrate your work ethic and enthusiasm. Let's try a few questions with the second resume entry and some other skills:

Supreme Project Planning — Budget analyst and Technical advisor — Apr 2018–Current

Duties consisted of allocating resources for the implementation of projects. Retrofit data was analyzed in order to gain approval for upgrades.

Highlighted skills

- Retrofit planning.
- Analysis.
- Auditing.
- Budgeting.

In this scenario you are looking to obtain a position as a Project planning leader with a small local firm, specializing in technology upgrades. They've asked you the following:

1. **"What are your greatest professional strengths?"**

"I feel that I have a good head for project analysis and logic. I have planned a number of retrofits and I was lucky enough to have someone who mentored me on auditing, budget allocation, preparing for pitfalls, and creating milestones in each project to assure they go as smoothly as possible. I've taken that information and refined those techniques as I have learned, moving along, and it shows in the work I can do today."

2. **"Why should we hire you?"**

"As a company that plans retrofits for their clientele, I think this job would not only be a good fit for me but I can be an asset. Project planning gives me a deep, personal satisfaction. It is challenging, requires forethought, and a dedication to the planned phases from start until the project completion. I feel I can bring my personal enthusiasm and strong work ethic into play and become a useful asset to this company."

3. "What do you know about the company?"

"I know a little about the company from what I have read on the website and from word of mouth. I know you install Data security solutions locally and the company has been growing, thus this has piqued my interest to apply myself and potentially grow my skills while sharing in the company's success."

These are just a few examples. With a little bit of Google magic, you can print yourself up a list of common questions and prepare some stories for each in a jiffy. You will want to make at least 2 answers for every question. Get a box and some index cards and you can make some reminder cards with a few pertinent words to remind you of each story. This way before the interview you can be rehearsed and ready!

We aren't done. In our next chapter we will discuss the STAR framework and how it pertains to telling your stories. Having the story handy, the STAR framework can help you deliver important information so you can ace that interview.

Are you ready? Let's discuss the STAR framework.

CHAPTER 4: STAR FRAMEWORK

Now we've come to the meat of the book. You've collected your skills and you've begun building up a cache of stories you would like to have ready for your interview. We've been telling you about the STAR framework, let's get a little more specific about it before we continue.

Designed primarily for dealing with behavioral interview questions, STAR is a means to make sure your stories are communicating what you wish them to. Once memorized, it is easily applicable, and with practice you will never seem surprised during an interview again!

The STAR framework consists of breaking down your stories into 4 parts. These parts are as follows:

- **Situation** — This is your background setting and the initial problem. For instance, "I was a Solutions Engineer at Qualitycorp and we were facing a difficult issue. Our customer needed to transfer his backup data to his new version of our software. His data, however, was from a legacy version of the software and not compatible."
- **Task** — This is simply a description of what you were trying to accomplish and why. By example, you might say, "This customer had not used us in a

while and due to a change in management they wanted their software up to date. This was a huge sale and so we needed to find a way to make this happen."
- **Action** — This is the approach you took for resolving the issue. "First, I asked for a data sample and after signing a non-disclosure agreement this was done. I found out this COULD be done with some older versions of the software we had in-house but it would be a time-consuming process. Seeing this as an opportunity, I spoke with one of our Sales Technicians and told them what needed to be done."
- **Result** — This is where you will describe what came as a result of your actions. "We scheduled a meeting with the Client and advised them that while the data can be transferred, due to the differences in the software after so many years it would likely require one of our in-house technicians to bring their software up to date. They agreed it would be necessary and as a bonus, the rapport I'd established with the client meant we were able to demonstrate and sell other software this client could use. I know this because I was actually sent to do the upgrade."

By taking your story components and arranging them in this format you can easily highlight the skills you wish to communicate. In our resolution we demonstrated that a rapport had been built, showing good customer service and that the company felt the level of expertise displayed with the product made this candidate a good fit for the database upgrade. The action demonstrated a logical approach to the technology and knowledge of the product, as well. We also mentioned working together with Sales, which shows good networking skills. With STAR, it's easy to highlight the skills and personality aspects that you wish, it just takes a little practice. That said, here are some tips for when you are creating your own STAR stories.

Tips for creating STAR stories

1. Situation — Set up at least 3 of your favorite career stories that you can readily adapt as needed.

2. Task — When describing the situation and your motivation, pay attention to the following:

- Tailor your answer as much to the position you are applying for. The better the story fit the more effective it will be during your interview.
- Don't forget you are there to show off your skills. Use more, "I did this, I did that" type sentences

rather than making everything a team effort. This is not the time to be humble (but don't go overboard, of course).

3. Action — This is where you are demonstrating your approach to problem-solving. Remember:

- Be detailed but try not to let stories go over 3 or 4 minutes unless prompted.
- Make mention of particular skills that helped you to surmount the issue.
- Don't make light of the obstacle. Tell it like it was and highlight your thought process as much as possible.

4. Result — When you are highlighting the end result of your actions in regards to the problem, a few things to keep in mind:

- If you learned something new that you have kept and used with other issues, this is a great way to end the story. Showing that you collect lessons to build your skills further shows the kind of character that gets people hired.
- If your solution built a profit, streamlined a project, or saved a customer, be sure to mention that. "We were able to cut costs by 10%," for instance. "By changing the implementation plan

we were able to finish the project 2 weeks early, providing us time to demonstrate further products to the client." Interviewers like to hear statements with impact so don't sell yourself short.

Now that we have described the system in more detail and provided a few tips to help you customize your responses, we'll discuss the usage of "action verbs" for giving yourself some stronger words you may use when communicating your skills. Following that, we are going to go into some of those tough interview questions so you can see some sample answers and maybe that will inspire you to tailor some of your stories.

Without further ado, let's proceed to Chapter 5, "Action Verbs Tell a Story!"

CHAPTER 5: ACTION VERBS TELL A STORY

Once you are familiar with the STAR framework for telling a story, adding a little punch to it with strong action verbs is a great way to enhance their delivery. Active language can make all the difference in a story or resume and action verbs are a great way to take advantage of this.

Not familiar with action verbs? Let's go a little into some verb-variance so we can empower and polish some of your work in preparation for those interviews!

Action verbs are nice and direct and extremely useful. While you can make your sentences long and complex, it isn't always as good for storytelling or for your resume.

If you doubt the power of the action verb, take a moment and give a nod to a famous quote from Julius Caesar: *Veni, vidi, vici.* "I came, I saw, I conquered."

There is a lot to be said for wording things just right! So how can you employ a little of this into your STAR skills? Mainly, you are going to be taking standard sentences out of your resume and descriptions as you write them, so that when you deliver or speak them it is more concise.

"I worked in a supervisory capacity on Project X."

"I supervised Project X."

While the first version sounds "fancier" in some ways, it has a lot of fat on it that you don't need. This can be important if you are shortening the length of a story or if you need to convey the facts quickly and professionally without going overboard. Mind you, those with a lot of customer service skills will tell you that the flowery phrases are useful. Even in a Corporate environment they work for certain ends, but in interviewing you want to be clear, concise, and brief.

We've compiled a list of action verbs along with some examples to show how they can really add a little zing into your delivery.

Action verb examples for various skills

Customer service

1. **Interface** — This one is quick, useful, and looks sounds sharp on resumes. Which do you like more on a resume?

"I provided customer service skills and managed escalations."

"Customer interface and escalation management."

2. **Persuade** — Chopping down sentence descriptions is all about the words you choose. In an interview you might say:

"Sometimes I had to convince customers to see the bigger picture."

"I'd persuade them to see the bigger picture."

3. **Encourage** — This one sounds nice and professional. Here is a contrast example:

"Sometimes I had to gently push a client towards a particular solution."

"Sometimes I'd encourage clients to a particular solution."

Creative thinking

1. **Originate** — Aside from relating to something's beginning, "originate" may be used in lieu of "create" and it sounds pretty snappy.

"I decided to originate a solution."

2. **Introduce** — Try using this outside of its standard social usage.

"I introduced the idea of trying _____."

3. **Establish** — This one is a nice one to throw around. Compare the following:

"I developed a new way to do this."

"I established a new standard."

Finance

1. **Allocate** — Not just applying to finance. There are a number of ways you can use this action verb. Check out the difference it makes:

"We needed to make sure we had the proper resources for this solution."

"We needed to allocate the proper resources for this solution."

2. **Project** — Another nice power verb. Compare the following sentences:

"In my position I often had to determine the anticipated costs for the creation of our budget."

"One of my roles was projecting costs to determine our budget."

3. **Quantify** — This one is tricky to inset until you have had a little practice but it can certainly shorten and polish a sentence.

"Part of my job was to figure out how much equipment and trained professionals we would need for a project."

"Part of my job was to quantify equipment and manpower involved in a project."

Leadership

1. **Administer** — This is one you can use quite often. As it is used to say, "manage and run," it is quite useful in describing leadership roles. Note the contrast:

"In this project I acted as the manager."

"I administered the project."

2. **Delegate** — Another good leadership role. Try to get in the habit of using this one when you can whenever you had to split up tasks or authority.

"My role was to take a project, break it down into smaller tasks, and delegate the various tasks to our most qualified personnel."

3. **Motivate** — Use instead of "encourage," for instance. This third entry in our leadership words comes in handy. Compare:

"My job was to encourage the Team in their efforts through supervision to meet our quota."

"I would motivate the team in a supervisory capacity to ensure we met our quota."

Technical

1. **Troubleshooting** — This is one that you probably use a lot if you are a seasoned tech. If you are just getting started, be sure to add it to your resumes and stories. This is the difference:

"My job was finding what was wrong with the software."

"My job was troubleshooting the software."

2. **Engineer** — Whenever you need to say that you put something together, try employing the word "engineer."

"I engineered a solution for the issue."

3. **Operated** — Do you work with machinery that requires special training? Compare these two methods of communicating the facts:

"I worked using the 3270 emulator mainframe."

"I operated the 3270 emulator mainframe."

We hope these examples will give you a better idea of how you can play around with language to sharpen your descriptions. Don't be intimidated to give one or more of these recommendations a try.

In our next chapter, we are going to take some of the principles we are utilizing here a step further as we teach you how to answer some of the trickiest questions found in interviews and how to deliver your own stories STAR style!

CHAPTER 6: INTERVIEW QUESTIONS AND ANSWERS

Now that we have a good idea of how the STAR framework is constructed and populated with action verbs, it is time to give you a taste of this system in action.

In this chapter we are going to cover a few core questions you will likely be asked verbatim or in variations specific to the field of work you are applying for. The core questions we will be covering are as follows:

- **Category:** Crises **Interview request:** "Describe how you handle difficult situations."
- **Category:** Clients **Interview request:** "Describe a time you were able to handle a difficult client."
- **Category:** Failure to Deliver **Interview request:** "Describe a time when you were not able to deliver on a promise."
- **Category:** Future **Interview request:** "Where do you see yourself in 5 years?"
- **Category:** Innovation **Interview request:** "Describe a situation in which you innovated a process for efficiency improvements."

As you can see, these questions cover a wide range of potential information about you that will be of interest to

Interviewers. We're going to demonstrate how the STAR technique makes questions of these sorts change from "intimidating" to "career building" with just a little preparation and application of STAR. Furthermore, we are going to address what these questions are supposed to say about you. Intrigued? Let's get started!

Crises

"Describe how you handle difficult situations."

The reasoning behind this question is simple enough but the question can jostle you a bit if you are not expecting it. So what are Employers looking for when they ask you this question? This question can tell potential Employers the following:

- Your answer can demonstrate how you deal with situations when they get beyond your scope of comfort. This is extremely important.
- This question can produce a candid response due to its "surprise" nature (unless you are properly prepared, of course!).
- Your current skill-level of communications with a bit of subtext (are you emphasizing certain parts of the story. For instance, are you focused on the behavior of co-workers? Are you sticking to the facts? Does the outcome suggest you performed

with confidence or that you "got lucky?" The STAR technique will come in very handy for this.
- This question can potentially test your honesty. Do NOT, under any circumstances, create a fictional scenario. Hiring Managers can spot this very quickly and they won't consider hiring you. Impress them instead with a little preparation and simple facts.

Other variants of this question:

- "Can you tell me about a difficult problem on the job which you dealt with in the past?"
- "Can you tell us about a time when you made a mistake on the job and had to correct it?"
- "Can you tell us about a time you had a task which was much more difficult than anticipated and what you did about it?"

Variants to this question are essentially still gauging the same core-concepts and mastery of STAR can help you to quickly amend your answers while retaining the basics you have prepared. How would you answer this sort of question utilizing the STAR technique? You will need to identify a story (or even better, multiple stories you can use), and work on polishing them with STAR.

For our example, let's say that a woman named Jan is preparing herself for this question. Jan has been asked, *"Can you tell me about a difficult problem on the job which you dealt with in the past?"* Having initially prepared for *"Describe how you handle difficult situations."* Jan immediately recalls a story from her previous job.

The verbose version: In Jan's previous position, she was providing Technical support to enterprise-level companies. All of these were large-level clients and one in particular was complaining that their technical issue had not been resolved, that it had been 2 whole weeks, and this was impacting their production levels. Jan had escalated the case to their Development team, the highest level, which consisted of coders who can actually change the software. The Sales team was also adding pressure, citing this was close to the time when the client would be renewing and possibly purchasing more software from the company. What could Jan do? Upon emailing the manager of the development team, Jan was informed there was a queue for escalated cases and asked why this customer should have priority over others. Jan contacted Sales to find out how much revenue each escalated client was pulling for the company, creating a spreadsheet with the data which demonstrated this client was the companies third biggest customer. She forwarded this to the Development team's management as well as her own and was able to get them to re-prioritize the queue, keep the client happy, and Sales was able to negotiate a larger contract for the next year.

It is a good story but too long for most interviews. That's where Jan uses her own STAR skills to deliver it sharply and succinctly:

- **Situation**: "One of our largest-revenue clients had a technical issue that was not being addressed due to a large waiting queue of client issues."
- **Task**: "The challenge was getting the customer's issue placed on priority by demonstrating to the Development team's management that there was a good reason for putting this issue over other client's issues in the queue."
- **Action**: "As Sales was pushing for a solution as well, I utilized their assistance to demonstrate the company could potentially lose a lot of existing and potential income by failing to prioritize this client. I created a spreadsheet displaying current revenue and the suggestion this could help in prioritizing escalating issues, then I forwarded the spreadsheet to both my manager and to the Development team manager."

- **Results**: "The list that was created helped the Development manager to prioritize escalated cases based on revenue, our client was happy again and no longer at risk, and Sales was able to work their magic as well, resulting in more business!"

As you can see, a concise re-telling of the story gets across the facts and makes Jan look good. While this is more of a demonstration, adopting a 3-rd party STAR analysis, it shows the basics. Let's continue with another common interview request...

Clients

"Describe a time you were able to handle a difficult client."

This question is designed to ascertain information about your personality. How well you deal with others, especially when they are being difficult, can give the Interviewer an idea of the following:

- Your skills with diplomacy.
- Your communications skills in general.
- Whether or not you have a degree of empathy.
- If your management of problems is in line with company policies and practice.

- If you are easily pushed around by clients through a lack of confidence.

Other variants of this question:

- "Can you tell us about a time when you had to deal with an angry customer?"
- "Can you describe a time when you had to deal with a customer you could not appease?"
- "Have you ever had an angry customer resort to profanity? What was the situation and how did you react?"

How you deal with clients is a matter of huge importance. Not only does it help to ensure retention of existing (and sometimes rather difficult) customers, your skills in this area may also relate to management. If you fold under the stress of dealing with an angry customer then how can you expect to manage a team? If you have difficulty dealing with angry or aggressive clients, you could state that and advise you require training in this area, but in general most of us have dealt with this situation and will have a story or two that can convert into STAR format for an interview.

For example, George has worked as a customer service representative and technician for an internet service provider for the past few years and has a number of stories ready for just this sort of question. During an interview, the Interviewer requests him to "describe a time that he was able to handle a difficult client."

The verbose version: George has collected a number of stories and recalls a favorite of his. One of their customers, Mr. Pruitt, was known for being particularly difficult. Upon calling to receive assistance his call was answered by a newly trained technician and Mr. Pruitt, a frequent caller, demanded to speak to a more experienced technician. His call was transferred to George for handling. George took advantage of this moment to help train the new technician, connecting the new technician's headset to his own. George then answered the call and when Mr. Pruitt began voicing his frustrations and stated he was considering another service provider. George let him speak and listened, repeating points of frustration in his own words as Mr. Pruitt delivered them but careful never to speak over Mr. Pruitt. He said he understood Mr. Pruitt was frustrated and he would file a report that would help to avoid such things in the future at the close of their call. Mr. Pruitt calmed down and agreed to let George attempt to finally help with his issue. In the end, George had to escalate the case because he couldn't fix the issue, but he promised Mr. Pruitt to personally follow-up on the issue to ensure it would be resolved to his satisfaction. Once the issue was resolved he made a follow-up call to check on Mr. Pruitt, who was delighted with the service he received and had decided to keep giving them his business.

Another good story and many of us who have worked in customer service before recognize George's techniques. So, how do we STAR things up?

- **Situation:** One of our most notoriously difficult customers had an issue and was angry when he received a novice technician on the phone.
- **Task:** I needed to ensure that his issue was resolved and make sure he felt he was getting the care level he expects from his investment in our services, while potentially improving our current and growing standards of customer service.
- **Action:** I took the call but realized this was a good training opportunity for the novice. I connected his headset to mine and advised him to take notes. I empathized with Mr. Pruitt and let him vent his frustrations so he would calm down and let us work on the issue. As he vented them, I repeated primary concerns he had in my own words, to reassure him I was listening. When he calmed down, we worked on the issue and while it was beyond my training I was able to escalate his case

to a senior technician for resolution. I promised him I would follow up and messaged the senior technician to let me know if he resolved the issue quickly or if further follow-up calls were needed. The technician solved the issue and I contacted Mr. Pruitt later to ask if his issue was fixed and if he was happy with the service. I also filed a report of his concerns to our internal system for review for future consideration.
- **Results:** Mr. Pruitt advised me he was happy with our service, he would keep his business with us, and our novice technician received a good training lesson you can't quite get in a classroom environment.

While this STAR example is more verbose, it is necessary in this case. George showed he was not just dedicated to the customer, but to training his teammates, improving overall standards through the documentation of customer complaints, and he is willing to go the extra mile by giving a follow-up call. George may have nailed this interview by his answer to this question alone!

Failure to Deliver

"Describe a time when you were not able to deliver on a promise."

Even with preparation, the core of this question makes it one of the harder ones to answer. Nobody wants to admit they failed. What you have to do to manage this question with tact and confidence is simple. Realize that everyone fails from time to time and this is how you LEARN. That said, what they are trying to gauge with this question is the following:

- Are you accountable to your actions, rather than someone who will make excuses?
- Are you a mature enough employee to overlook your pride and ask for help when you need it?
- Do you treat failures as a personal blow or an experience which you can learn from? Everybody gains experience by failing at one time or another. Be honest but accentuate the lessons learned, not the loss.
- Your behavior when you tell the story. If you don't tell it concisely then it could indicate you may still have some slight accountability issues to work through.

Other variants of this question:

- "Can you tell us about a time when your actions caused you to miss or almost miss a deadline?"
- "Can you tell us about a time when you failed in your responsibilities?"

Remember, this is just to gauge how you DEAL with failure. This is to see what you have learned. So don't panic when you get this question because you will be prepared. Now that we have reminded you of the core function of these questions, let's give you an example of a story that works well with a little STAR wizardry (use your own, of course, this is just an example!).

The verbose version: Jan recalls an issue from when she was fairly new at a company and was asked if she could head a class to train other employees in some skills she had obtained in a previous position. She needed PowerPoint added to her system and some personal computers needed to be loaded with the software she was going to be training in. Jan was confident this would be the work of a day but failed to take into consideration the company waiting period of 3 days for the loading of new software. As she was new, she had not been aware of the policy, and due to her already-busy workload she put off creating the course for the middle of the week. On Tuesday, she found out about the policy from a co-worker, and in a panic she put in her request right away and told her manager about her mistake. Management helped to make sure the request would go through but advised Jan she would need to juggle this with her current workload for the week while still ensuring she could run the training class. While she was still able to create her class and train the other employees by getting ahead on her workload (utilizing some of her free time to stay late and by crafting the PowerPoint presentation at home), Jan took this experience as a lesson that proper preparation for responsibilities is paramount and to be more careful when managing her time.

What would be the STAR version of this scenario?

- **Situation:** "I'd been asked to prepare a class in an area of personal expertise that would be useful for my co-workers to have."
- **Task:** "Assuming all my necessary resources would be available and it was just a simple matter of making a PowerPoint and loading the software for them to follow along, I assumed the class to be of low priority, easily finished. Then I learned it takes 3 days to approve the necessary software for my class."

- **Action:** "I notified my Manager and told him I had put off the work without knowing about the policy, apologizing and admitting I should have checked to see that I would have everything I needed right away. I also spent some personal time working at home and staying in the office to ensure the workload would be met despite my mistaken priorities."
- **Results:** "I learned to prepare for my diverse workload more effectively and reaffirmed to myself that the job is more important than my personal pride. It is always better to admit your mistakes and ask for help than to miss an important deadline."

It should be noted: Be sure when you are crafting a STAR type answer for this question that you select your story carefully. The goal is to select a story when you learned something from a mistake, so don't use just any mistake and avoid any that may have ended poorly.

Future

"Where do you see yourself in 5 years?"

While your knee-jerk reaction is going to be giving a generic answer like, "Why working here, of course!" This is a question you will need to think out and answer thoughtfully. What they are trying to determine from your response are the following things:

- Your ambitions. Are they something you have thought out? Are you extremely ambitious or simply looking to retain the same role but enjoy access to resources to develop your skills that are specific to this company?
- Your planning skills. Is there something about this job that fits with your plan for the future? Skills you can pick up so you can move ahead in a specific field, for instance.

Other variants of this question:

- "Where do you see yourself in the near future?"
- "What kind of future do you envision for yourself here?"

Now that you have an idea of what they are looking for, this question is not so hard at all. Let's visit George again for an example.

The verbose version: George has been asked, "Where do you see yourself in the near future?" Having planned for this question and having devoted time to thinking it out, George knows he wants this particular position due to some specific hardware technologies this company manufactures and manages, which fascinate him. He feels he would enjoy working with this technology so he can eventually understand the technology completely, both at the hardware and software level. This is because he dreams of eventually creating the next generation of these machines as well as the software for them.

So how does George formulate this into a STAR response?

- **Situation:** "You'd like to know where I see myself in 5 years. The answer is here and I'll tell you why."
- **Task:** "I'm fascinated with technologies that are specific to this company and so I feel I would be a good fit for this company and this job would be a good fit for me."
- **Action:** "The reasons behind this are: working here lets me work almost exclusively with this technology so I can learn it at both a hardware and software level until I am an expert in my field."
- **Results**: "As a result of this, while working hard with these technologies I envision eventually understanding them at a Developer level so I can one day help to produce the next generations of this technology. I think I could get close to realizing this dream here because I'd be working

hard with a technology and company that is already a passion of mine."

George has communicated quite clearly that he is familiar with and passionate about the very technologies produced by this company. It shows he has chosen this position with forethought, combining something he enjoys with a well-thought out plan for his future. Many people go into interviews without having an idea how the specifics of a particular job could help them. Be sure to plan so you don't fall into this category. You can do much better for yourself with a little planning.

Innovation

"Describe a situation in which you innovated a process for efficiency improvements."

This is one of those questions where you really get to shine. Have you been in a job situation where you improved upon a process that was becoming dated? Have you streamlined a task by changing one portion of the sequence? When employers ask you this question they are trying to ascertain:

- If you have initiative.
- If you are constantly trying to improve processes in a way that can save the company money or

increase productivity.
- If you have leadership potential.
- If your ideas are clever.

Other variants of this question:

- "Can you tell us about a time where your initiative solved a problem or streamlined a process?"
- "Have you ever analyzed and improved upon an existing workflow practice at a company?"

Odds are, if you think about it a little, there are a surprising number of times where you were performing your duties and found a clever shortcut that proved beneficial enough to keep. Let's visit Jan and see how she answered this question. Now, as Jan had already advised about her innovation with the revenue spreadsheet, you might think she would not be prepared when asked if she had ever innovated a process to improve efficiency. Not so! She anticipated many different types of interview questions and thus had more than one scenario for the most common questions. This comes highly recommended. Let's see what she had to say.

The verbose version: Jan was working one day and having a nice lunch when a co-worker she was dining with asked if she wanted to see a concert for a band she liked. She wanted to go but knew she needed to check with her manager first and possibly spend a bit of time asking other co-workers about trading a shift for that day or even a day off. That's when she got an idea. On the network, there was a spreadsheet shared by all her co-workers, where one would mark their current days off for vacation, training, and other reasons. Why not make a "switch" sheet? Basically, a spreadsheet where someone could mark on the calendar days when they wanted to switch shifts with someone else or to trade a day off. Jan created an example sheet on the remaining minutes of her lunch sheet and spoke with the manager about it. Her manager liked the idea, as it allowed Jan and her co-workers a way to have a little control of their own schedules while ensuring coverage. It also gave the manager a little more time to manage other responsibilities beyond schedule change requests. Jan's "Swap sheet" worked out nicely in practice and was adopted by other teams later due to its popularity and efficiency.

Now, let's give that story the STAR treatment:

- **Situation**: "I had an idea on my lunch break to streamline our scheduling process."
- **Task**: "I recognized that my co-workers and I shared a problem with management. Juggling our schedules. We already had a solution in place to

indicate which person had which days off but wanted to take it a step further."
- **Action**: "I drafted an example spreadsheet, to depict co-workers posting times they wanted off in one color so everyone could see at a glance who was looking to change shifts or day's off. I showed my manager and she liked the idea."
- **Results**: "The self-service shift change or "Swap sheet" as it came to be called worked out nicely. It saved time and minimized manager utilization for minor changes in shift or requested time off. While it didn't work for all teams, many other teams are still using it. It's a little idea I'm still quite proud of."

It's a nice story and a great example of a small innovation that saved a little time for a number of people. Accrue that time-saved over a year and you would be surprised at how much "little" solutions can do for a company. Keep that in mind when you draft your own STAR stories. You don't have to rock the foundation of a company to make changes that can be useful. Look deep and you'll likely see you've made a lot of innovations that would fit well for this question and you can reflect upon proudly.

Now that we have given you a number of good examples for utilizing STAR for your experience stories, we're going to take that a step further and show you how to utilize STAR for building a stellar resume that shows potential employers EXACTLY what you have to offer. Are you ready? Let's proceed to Chapter 7, "Creating your own STAR resume!"

CHAPTER 7: CREATING YOUR STAR RESUME

Well, now that you've got a collection of stories, how do we bring the same kind of impact we are getting in our interviews directly to the resume? The answer, of course, is bullet points! With a little bit of planning you can bring some STAR power to your resume. Let's get started!

Steps for giving your resume STAR power

1. Collect a handful of skills you would like demonstrated in your resume and you feel companies are looking for in your line of work. Select 5 or 6 so we can keep the resume brief and concise, you can always modify it later.

Example Skills — Technical support

- **Troubleshooting.**
- **Product knowledge.**
- **Customer interface.**
- **Co-worker training.**
- **Call leading.**

2. Identify scenarios where a demonstration of these skills was called for during your work at these previous positions.

3. Apply the STAR framework to these stories. This will make for a smaller story and make it easier when we are making bullet points.

4. Lastly, divide up your bullet points in such a manner they are associated with the skills you are showcasing. For instance, you might have an example like this:

Gravitas ISP — Customer Service Representative — Apr. 2017–Apr. 2018

Provided customer service in a fast-paced and dynamic environment. Skills utilized included the following:

- **Troubleshooting** — Utilized creative troubleshooting skills ensuring connectivity as well as ensuring general usage of the Gravitas webpage maker. Escalation rate was at less than five percent of calls.
- **Product knowledge** — Attended both mandatory and optional quarterly training to ensure an expert-level understanding of the products Gravitas offers.
- **Customer interface** — Provided empathy and professional courtesy, delivered with a smile, developing rapport with a number of customers who frequently called for support.

- **Co-worker training** — Utilized in training co-workers as a result of product expertise. A number of technicians trained were selected for higher tiers of support as well.
- **Call leading** — Kept calls at a minimum of time by leading the call, even with problematical customers, so that no time was wasted and issues could be resolved in a timely and satisfactory manner and scoring in the top ten percent of call metrics.

This can be done with a wide variety of skills so your resume can better reflect, at a glance, the skills you feel are most marketable. An example resume in this vein would appear as follows:

George Techyguy

1234 Generic street

Dallas, Texas 76049

george@fakeemail.net

Motivation: Seeking employment in a dynamic environment to increase my growing technical skills and establish my long-term career.

Work history:

Supreme Project Planning — Budget analyst and Technical advisor

Apr 2018 – Current

Duties consisted of allocating resources for the implementation of projects. Retrofit data was analyzed in order to gain approval for upgrades.

- **Retrofit planning** — As a technical advisor and budget analyst I created projects from the ground up, focusing on milestones to keep each product scheduled concisely.
- **Analysis** — Provided independent assessment of each client's needs in order to retrofit legacy technology to current, appreciable levels.
- **Auditing** — Analysis was provided after an intensive audit to identify current hardware and that client environment met minimum standards for upgrade compliance.
- **Budgeting** — Upon audit completion, initial analysis was performed and estimations of hardware and labor costs were calculated for our Sales department, who could then close the deal when an agreeable profit margin was met. My polling of vendors provided a ten percent increase

in Sales margin due to the availability of comparable hardware at a lesser price.

Gravitas ISP —- Customer Service Representative Apr. 2017–Apr. 2018

Duties consisted of providing customer service and basic troubleshooting in a busy call center environment for customers using our internet service provider and web software. Skills most utilized include:

- **Troubleshooting** — Utilized creative troubleshooting skills ensuring connectivity as well as ensuring general usage of the Gravitas webpage maker. Escalation rate was at less than five percent of calls.
- **Product knowledge** — Attended both mandatory and optional quarterly training to ensure an expert-level understanding of the products Gravitas offers.
- **Customer interface** — Provided empathy and professional courtesy, delivered with a smile, developing rapport with a number of customers who frequently called for support.
- **Co-worker training** — Utilized in training co-workers as a result of product expertise. A number

of technicians trained were selected for higher tiers of support as well.

- **Call leading** — Kept calls at a minimum of time by leading the call, even with problematical customers, so that no time was wasted and issues could be resolved in a timely and satisfactory manner and scoring in the top ten percent of call metrics.

Sellingstuff.net — Sales technician

Apr.2016–Apr. 2017

Duties consisted of demonstration of hardware products as well sales retention and new client acquisition. Skills most employed in this position were:

- **Client acquisition** — Due to a high success rate with customers, I was one of the top 3 in the company for initial contact selection.
- **Client retention** — By earning the clients trust and gaining rapport, my retention rate of existing customers was at ninety-five percent.
- **Product demonstrations** — Attended training which enabled me to provide detailed product demonstrations, while addressing questions from interested clients about product usage and upgrade path for future builds.

Further information is available upon request

As you can see, George's resume has a nice polish to it where upon a prospective employer can see, at a glance, a number of useful skills and how they were employed in various parts of George's career. You will also note this not only highlights the important skills but it also helps to avoid sending out a resume with your entire career history. While it is good to make one of those (it really depends on your level of experience, the position, and the company's attention to detail), in most cases your last few positions will be fine.

If you are worried, you can always make a more extensive resume copy to keep handy or for answering questions about the earlier parts of your work history.

Now that we have gone into creating a STAR resume, let's see what goes into making a STAR cover letter. By utilizing an eye-catching cover letter that showcases information about you then you can help to set your resume apart from the many others. Make sure you create a cover letter, after all, you've got to get that interview first before you can use your clever answers. Take the few extra minutes making the cover letter. It is worth it! Let's proceed to Chapter 8 and show you how to craft one!

CHAPTER 8: STAR COVER LETTERS

Developing cover letters using the STAR system is a great way to stick out and not very difficult to do. In this chapter we are going to detail the steps for creating your own, while providing an example cover letter after a breakdown of the steps. Are you ready?

Let's get started!

Steps for creating your own STAR cover letter

1. Select the three skills you feel are your most powerful. We are going to be basing your cover letter story on these and incorporating them throughout in order to show off your expertise in that important moment when an employer receives your resume.

2. Select 3 stories which exhibit your usage of these key skills. We are going to break them down and include them in your cover letter!

So, let's say that Gravitas ISP is hiring a technical trainer in their product, "Gravitas Webpage Maker." You want to get them to look at your resume so you are going to open with a brief bio and information as to why you would like to work at Gravitas.

From:

George Techyguy — Gravitas Products specialist

1234 Generic street

Dallas, Texas 76049

George@fakeemail.net

To:

Jan Pritchard

Human resources department

Gravitas

Hello Jan,

I was writing in regards to your position providing advanced training for Gravitas Webpage Maker. I feel I would be a good fit for this as I have worked with the product for a number of your vendors. As such, I have accumulated extensive training in the product since its earliest build and also real-time expertise in the following:

- **Product knowledge** — As a number of customers have needed both website and support, with my 10 plus years of experience with this product, I have provided training, support, and utilized it in the creation of more than 250 successful websites.

- **Co-worker training** — At Company A I was tasked to implement training and in the end succeeded in improving upon the previous training standards for the product. Implementing a course consisting of core subjects, this was put into place as a company standard that is in use to this day.

- **Troubleshooting** — Due to training and constant product usage, I have unlocked and am able to use a number of Developer level functions, which have been used to greatly effect advanced troubleshooting and an existing rapport with many current technicians at Gravitas.

I hope you will take the time to review my resume in consideration for this position. This is a product I love and I feel my dedication and experience can help me to become an asset with your company. Thank you in advance for your time and consideration.

Regards,

George Techyguy

Now, as you can see in this cover letter, we opened with reasons why we feel George would be a good fit for this position. By taking 3 skills and highlighting them with examples, we are also providing valuable data demonstrating George is a strong candidate before Jan has even viewed his resume. Not too shabby, eh?

The easy-to-remember format is as follows:

1. **Introduction** — Why you feel you would be a good fit for this position. You can include a quick intro as well but don't overdo it, we want a quick intro which then segues into step 2.

2. **3 Skills that pertain to this position** — Take your 3 best stories that illustrate your prime skills. This part can take a little reflection. If you have been collecting your stories as you read along this should not be too difficult.

3. **Thank you and closing** — Reiterate that you think your skills demonstrate you are a good potential candidate. Thank them for their time and for considering further exploration of your skills through the reading of your resume!

Just in case you are still getting a handle on the STAR system, let's do one last example of converting a story into STAR.

George would like to relate a story for one of his skills as part of the 3 for the cover letter. The skill being "diplomacy." He recalls a scenario where one of the customers, more technically minded than most, was dreaded because he would inevitably refuse to try troubleshooting steps required for escalation. George let him vent, while occasionally discussing technical aspects of the product with the customer in order for him to feel respected as a peer and more amenable to following the basic support steps. Once calmed, it turned out that one of the recommended steps gave George the information he needed to solve the problem. The issue was solved without escalation and George found he had developed a rapport with the customer and shared his technique with co-workers, which would become a training standard to help diffuse many a difficult call in the times ahead.

So, what's the STAR breakdown?

- **Situation** — At Company A there is a problematical customer with enough tech savvy to get himself in trouble. He needs to be helped.

- **Task** — To calm the customer enough that it would be possible to lead the call to a solution and retain the customer's business.
- **Action** — George employed Customer service skills such as empathy, listening, and repeating the customer's frustrations to show understanding, and the building of rapport through technical discussion to acknowledge the customer was not a novice with the product.
- **Result** — George was able to diffuse the customer's anger and solve the problem without escalation. This resulted in building a rapport with the customer which previously no one had.

After the STAR Breakdown, you can take some of the fat off for your bullet point:

- At company A I utilized customer service training involving listening and repeating a customer's complaints to acknowledge them, building rapport through treating the customer respectfully for learning the tech, and finally leading the call to its resolution once the customer had calmed. The issue fixed, the customer was happy, and the technique used to calm him was shared. A recording of the call was made part of the initial training as a standard for dealing with difficult clients.

We hope this revisiting of the STAR method for creating cover letters was useful. Remember. Intro, 3 stories, and then Thanks! It is the easy formula that can get you the perfect job. Customizing your cover letters to the companies you are looking to work for is that little extra effort that can pay off big. Many people tend to skip the cover letter or worse, they end up sending a boring and generic cover letter. If you want them to know you are interested then make sure you take the time to customize the cover letter before you send your resume. It truly can make all of the difference.

CONCLUSION

We would like to thank you for taking the time to read, "*The STAR Method Explained.*" In this book, we went over techniques to audit your skills, create stories, and then how to utilize the STAR format to make them shine.

When you get a chance, be sure to Google the most common interview "trick" questions. Develop a list for yourself, which you can print and utilize before any interviews to test yourself. If you start compiling stories for your interviews then you will soon find there are not going to be many you cannot adapt your source information to address.

While we realize everybody's stories are different, just stick to the system: Situation, Task, Action, and Results. Break your stories down to this format and your answers in the interviews will come out well-polished. Don't forget that a card box and index cards can help you keep a career's-worth of your unique stories ready for review before that important interview.

Also, be sure to create your new resume and start customizing your cover letters.

The job you've been waiting for is out there and soon you'll be getting it.

Made in the USA
Las Vegas, NV
18 July 2022